CREATING
A COMMONWEALTH

A Guide To Your State Government

Pennsylvania House of Representatives

ACKNOWLEDGEMENTS

Creating a Commonwealth: A Guide to Your State Government is intended to provide an educational and informational resource for citizens of the Commonwealth. It was produced by the Pennsylvania House of Representatives under the direction of the Office of the Parliamentarian.

The Office of the Parliamentarian wishes to thank the many individuals who contributed to the production of Creating a Commonwealth and extends special recognition to Judith J. Rogers, Julie Seiler and Caryn Green for organizing and editing the information presented here.

TABLE OF CONTENTS

CREATING
A COMMONWEALTH

A Guide To Your State Government

Pennsylvania House of Representatives

*"Think of your forefathers!
Think of your posterity!"*

3

– John Quincy Adams, speech, December 1802

<u>Creating a Commonwealth: A Guide to Your State Government</u> is intended to provide answers to many of the questions about how government works in Pennsylvania. It is easy to think of state government only in the present tense—what are the current laws, rules and customs and how do they affect the problems and situations facing today's citizens of the Commonwealth.

But readers of this book would be well-advised to heed Adams' words. Our history is the evolution of our government, and our future will depend on what is done or fails to be done by our present elected and appointed representatives.

The constitutional rights of the people of Pennsylvania, the manner in which we elect our legislators, governors and judges, and the boundaries within which those officials may act on behalf of the voters reflect the intentions of our forefathers and will have consequences to our posterity. It is the responsibility of contemporary society to examine the contributions of those who came before and to help determine the path future generations will take.

<u>Creating a Commonwealth</u> is a primer that gives the reader a glimpse at the very complex entity that is your state government. To the curious mind, some answers will lead to other questions. It is hoped that readers will seek out further information on topics of particular interest.

1. **WHAT WERE THE PRIMARY REASONS FOR THE ESTABLISHMENT OF THE UNITED STATES GOVERNMENT?**

   Our Founding Fathers expressed their reasons in the preamble to the Constitution: to "form a more perfect Union, establish Justice, insure domestic tranquility, provide for the common defense, promote the general Welfare, and secure the Blessings of Liberty to ourselves and our Posterity..."

2. **WHAT IS A REPUBLIC?**

   A republic is that form of government in which the administration of affairs is open to all the citizens. It is characterized by a constitutional form of government, especially a democratic one. A republican government is a government by representatives chosen by the people.

3. **WHAT IS A DEMOCRACY?**

   A democracy is government by the people. In a democracy, supreme power is vested in the people and exercised by them, either directly (absolute or pure democracy) or through elected representatives (representative democracy).

4. **IS THE UNITED STATES GOVERNMENT A REPUBLIC OR A DEMOCRACY?**

   It is both. The United States is a republic because we have a constitution, an elected leader rather than a monarch, and our citizens all work freely and equally toward the same cause—the preservation and operation of the nation.

   The United States government is also a representative democracy. An absolute or pure democracy would be unwieldy because of the country's large area and population.

5. WHAT IS THE "SUPREME LAW OF THE LAND"?

The United States Constitution, federal laws, and treaties are considered to be the "supreme law of the land." The judges of every state are bound by it, regardless of anything contrary in individual state constitutions or laws.

6. WHAT IS A COMMONWEALTH?

In reference to Pennsylvania, the word "commonwealth" is synonymous with "state." The term is of English derivation and implies a special devotion of the government to the common "weal," or the welfare of its citizens.

The colony of William Penn was known as the Quaker Commonwealth, and records show that those who framed the Pennsylvania constitutions from 1776 through 1878 continued this terminology. Interestingly, the state seal of Pennsylvania does not use the term, but as a matter of tradition it is the legal designation used in referring to the state.

7. HOW MANY COMMONWEALTHS ARE THERE IN THE UNITED STATES?

Four. In addition to Pennsylvania, Kentucky, Massachusetts, and Virginia are also considered commonwealths.

8. WHY IS PENNSYLVANIA CALLED THE "KEYSTONE STATE"?

This nickname for Pennsylvania first appeared shortly after the American Revolution and was in common usage by the early 1800s. It is believed that the original attribution referred to Pennsylvania's central geographic location among the Atlantic seaboard states. Modern use of the designation is justified in view of Pennsylvania's key position in the economic, social, and political development of the United States.

9. **HAS HARRISBURG ALWAYS BEEN THE CAPITAL OF PENNSYLVANIA?**

No. The Pennsylvania Colony established its first capital in 1643 at Tinicum Island in the Delaware River.

William Penn arrived in 1682 and convened the first General Assembly in Chester, which remained the capital until the following year. Philadelphia became the state capital when the Provincial Government was established there in 1683.

Lancaster became the capital on the first Monday of November 1799 and remained so until Harrisburg was designated as the seat of state government in 1812.

10. **HOW CAN THE LOCATION OF THE STATE CAPITAL BE CHANGED?**

The Constitution says that a law that would change the location of Pennsylvania's state capital would only be valid when voted on and approved by voters in a general election (see Article III, Section 28).

11. **WHAT PENNSYLVANIA CITIES WERE ONCE THE CAPITAL OF THIS COUNTRY?**

Philadelphia, Lancaster, and York. During the Revolutionary War, when General Washington was defeated by General Howe at Brandywine, it was decided to move the capital from Philadelphia because of the fear of attack. Congress adjourned and met in Lancaster for one day before moving to York. York remained the capital during the British occupation of Philadelphia from 1777 until 1778. The seat of government was transferred briefly to New York City and then returned to Philadelphia until 1800, when it moved to Washington, D.C.

12. **WHO WAS THE ONLY NATIVE PENNSYLVANIAN TO BE ELECTED PRESIDENT OF THE UNITED STATES?**

James Buchanan, born in Cove Gap, Franklin County, in 1791, was elected President of the United States in 1856.

The Pennsylvania Constitution is the foundation of our state government—the well from which liberty and justice spring forth. Our first Constitution was adopted in 1776 and was a framework for the U.S. Constitution, which did not take effect until 1789.

The articles and amendments of the Pennsylvania Constitution compose the fundamental law of the Commonwealth. It ensures basic rights to our citizens, outlines the structure of our government, and provides the rules by which our representatives are elected and how they conduct the business of the state.

While this section of the book focuses on the Pennsylvania Constitution, the answers to many of the questions in other sections come directly from this important document. For additional information, it is suggested that the reader refer to the Constitution as a supplement to this guide to Pennsylvania government. A copy of the Pennsylvania Constitution may be obtained from your state legislator.

DECLARATION OF RIGHTS

13. *WHAT ARE THE RIGHTS SET FORTH IN THE DECLARATION OF RIGHTS OF THE PENNSYLVANIA CONSTITUTION?*

The Declaration of Rights of the Pennsylvania Constitution predates and was a model for the Bill of Rights of the United States Constitution. It is primarily a list of "don'ts" for the General Assembly in that it prohibits the enactment of laws that would infringe on certain rights.

Those rights and prohibitions are set forth in the 28 sections of the declaration, as follows:

Section 1. Inherent Rights of Mankind

All men are born equally free and independent, and have certain inherent and indefeasible rights, among which are those of enjoying and defending life and liberty, of acquiring, possessing and protecting property and reputation, and of pursuing their own happiness.

Section 2. Political Powers

All power is inherent in the people, and all free governments are founded on their authority and instituted for their peace, safety, and happiness. For the advancement of these ends they have at all times an inalienable and indefeasible right to alter, reform or abolish their government in such manner as they may think proper.

Section 3. Religious Freedom

All men have a natural and indefeasible right to worship Almighty God according to the dictates of their own consciences; no man can of right be compelled to attend, erect or support any place of worship or to maintain any ministry against his consent; no human authority can, in any case whatever, control or interfere with the rights of conscience, and no preference shall ever be given by law to any religious establishments or modes of worship.

Section 4. Religion

No person who acknowledges the being of a God and a future state of rewards and punishments shall, on account of his religious sentiments, be disqualified to hold any office or place of trust or profit under this Commonwealth.

Section 5. Elections

Elections shall be free and equal; and no power, civil or military, shall at any time interfere to prevent the free exercise of the right of suffrage.

Section 6. Trial by Jury

Trial by jury shall be as heretofore, and the right thereof remain inviolate. The General Assembly may provide, however, by law, that a verdict may be rendered by not less than five-sixths of the jury in any civil case.

Section 7. Freedom of Press and Speech; Libels

The printing press shall be free to every person who may undertake to examine the proceeding of the Legislature or any branch of government, and no law shall ever be made to restrain the right thereof. The free communication of thoughts and opinions is one of the invaluable rights of man, and every citizen may freely speak, write and print on any subject, being responsible for the abuse of that liberty. No conviction shall be had in any prosecution for the publication of papers relating to the official conduct of officers or men in public capacity, or to any other matter proper for public investigation or information, where the fact that such publication was not maliciously or negligently made shall be established to the satisfaction of the jury; and in all indictments for libels the jury shall have the right to determine the law and the facts, under the direction of the court, as in other cases.

Section 8. Security From Searches and Seizures

The people shall be secure in their persons, houses, papers and possessions from unreasonable searches and seizures, and no warrant to search any place or seize any person or things shall issue without describing them as nearly as may be, nor without probable case, supported by oath or affirmation subscribed to by the affiant.

Section 9. Rights of Accused in Criminal Prosecutions

In all criminal prosecutions the accused hath a right to be heard by himself and his counsel, to demand the nature and cause of the accusation against him, to meet the witnesses face to face, to have compulsory process for obtaining witnesses in his favor, and, in prosecutions by indictment or information, a speedy public trial by an impartial jury of the vicinage; he cannot be compelled to give evidence against himself, nor can he be deprived of his life, liberty or property, unless by the judgment of his peers or the law of the land. The use of a suppressed voluntary admission or voluntary confession to impeach the credibility of a person may be permitted and shall not be construed as compelling a person to give evidence against himself.

Section 10. Eminent Domain; Initiation of Criminal Proceedings; Twice in Jeopardy

Except as hereinafter provided no person shall, for any indictable offense, be proceeded against criminally by information, except in cases arising in the land or naval forces, or in the militia, when in actual service, in time of war or public danger, or by leave of the court for oppression or misdemeanor in office. Each of the several courts of common pleas may, with the approval of the Supreme Court, provide for the initiation of criminal proceedings therein by information filed in the manner provided by law. No person shall, for the same offense, be twice put in jeopardy of life or limb; nor shall private property be taken or applied to public use, without authority of law and without just compensation being first made or secured.

Section 11. Open Courts; Suits Against the Commonwealth

All courts shall be open; and every man for an injury done him in his lands, goods, person or reputation shall have remedy by due course of law, and right and justice administered without sale, denial or delay. Suits may be brought against the Commonwealth in such manner, in such courts and in such cases as the Legislature may by law direct.

Section 12. Power of Suspending Laws

No power of suspending laws shall be exercised unless by the Legislature or by its authority.

Section 13. Bail, Fines and Punishments

Excessive bail shall not be required, nor excessive fines imposed, nor cruel punishments inflicted.

Section 14. Prisoners to be Bailable; Habeas Corpus

All prisoners shall be bailable by sufficient sureties, unless for capital offenses when the proof is evident or presumption great; and the privilege of the writ of habeas corpus shall not be suspended, unless when in the case of rebellion or invasion the public safety may require it.

Section 15. Special Criminal Tribunals

No commission shall issue creating special temporary criminal tribunals to try particular individuals or particular classes of cases.

Section 16. Insolvent Debtors

The person of a debtor, where there is not strong presumption of fraud, shall not be continued in prison after delivering up his estate for the benefit of his creditors in such manner as shall be prescribed by law.

Section 17. Ex Post Facto Laws; Impairment of Contracts

No ex post facto law, nor any law impairing the obligation of contracts, or making irrevocable any grant of special privilege or immunities, shall be passed.

Section 18. Attainder

No person shall be attained of treason or felony by the Legislature.

Section 19. Attainder Limited

No attainder shall work corruption of blood, nor, expect during the life of the offender, forfeiture of estate to the Commonwealth.

Section 20. Right of Petition

The citizens have a right in a peaceable manner to assemble together for their common good, and to apply to those invested with the powers of government for redress of grievances or other proper purposes by petition, address or remonstrance.

Section 21. Right to Bear Arms

The right of the citizens to bear arms in defense of themselves and the State shall not be questioned.

Section 22. Standing Army; Military Subordinate to Civil Power

No standing army shall, in time of peace, be kept up without the consent of the Legislature, and the military shall in all cases and at all times be in strict subordination to the civil power.

Section 23. Quartering of Troops

No soldier shall in time of peace be quartered in any house without the consent of the owner, nor in time of war but in a manner to be prescribed by law.

Section 24. Titles and Offices

The Legislature shall not grant any title of nobility or heredity distinction, nor create any office the appointment to which shall be for a longer term than during good behavior.

Section 25. Reservation of Powers in People

To guard against transgressions of the high powers which we have delegated, we declare that everything in this article is excepted out of the general powers of government and shall forever remain inviolate.

Section 26. No Discrimination by Commonwealth or Political Subdivisions.

Neither the Commonwealth nor any political subdivision thereof shall deny to any person the enjoyment of any civil right, nor discriminate against any person in the exercise of any civil right.

Section 27. Natural Resources and the Public Estate

The people have a right to clean air, pure water, and to the preservation of the natural, scenic, historic and esthetic values of the environment. Pennsylvania's public natural resources are the common property of all the people, including generations yet to come. As trustee of these resources, the Commonwealth shall conserve and maintain them for the benefit of all the people.

Section 28. Sexual Discrimination

Equality of rights under the law shall not be denied or abridged in the Commonwealth of Pennsylvania because of the sex of the individual.

SEPARATION OF POWERS

14. *WHAT IS MEANT BY "SEPARATION OF POWERS"?*

The Pennsylvania Constitution provides in separate articles for three branches of government—legislative, executive, and judicial. There is a significant difference in the type of power granted to each branch.

The second article of the Constitution gives "legislative power of the Commonwealth" to the General Assembly, which includes both the Senate and the House of Representatives.

The fourth article gives the Governor "supreme executive power."

Judicial power is addressed in the fifth article, which establishes "a unified judicial system consisting of the Supreme Court, the Superior Court, the Commonwealth Court, courts of common pleas, community courts, municipal and traffic courts in the City of Philadelphia, and other such courts as may be provided by law and justices of the peace."

This three-way separation of government is intended to keep each branch independent of the others, providing a system of checks and balances that offers protection against the concentration of power within one branch.

AMENDMENTS

15. HOW CAN THE CONSTITUTION BE AMENDED?

Amendments to the Pennsylvania Constitution may be proposed in either the Senate or the House of Representatives but must pass in both by a majority vote of the members elected.

Three months before the next general election, the proposed amendment is published in at least two newspapers in every county. After the election, the amendment must again be approved through a majority vote of the members of the General Assembly. The amendment is again published and voted on by the entire electorate. If passed by a majority vote, the amendment becomes part of the Constitution.

No individual amendment can be submitted more often than once in five years, and when two or more amendments are submitted at once, they are voted on separately (see Article XI, Section 1).

16. WHAT ABOUT IN AN EMERGENCY?

The procedure to amend the Constitution is simplified somewhat when a major emergency threatens the safety and welfare of the Commonwealth.

An emergency amendment can be proposed in the Senate or the House of Representatives at any regular or special session and must be passed by at least two-thirds of the members of both legislative bodies. The proposed amendment is then published in at least two newspapers in every county and is then voted upon by the electorate at least one month after being agreed to by the General Assembly. If there are two or more emergency amendments, they are voted on separately (see Article XI, Section 1).

17. HAS THIS EMERGENCY AMENDMENT PROCEDURE EVER BEEN USED?

Yes. Because of widespread damage to many parts of the state caused by Hurricane Agnes in the summer of 1972, a special session of the General Assembly was convened on August 14, 1972. A joint resolution was passed to amend the Constitution allowing the Assembly to enact laws providing tax rebates, credits, exemptions, grants-in-aid, state supplementations and other special provisions to individuals, corporations, associations, and nonprofit institutions, including private schools.

The purpose of this emergency amendment was to alleviate the danger, damage, suffering, and hardship as a result of a great storm or flood of September 1971 and June 1972. It was approved by the electorate on November 7, 1972.

This procedure was followed again in the regular sessions of 1975 and 1977, adding the years of 1974, 1975, and 1977. These additional emergency amendments were also approved by the electorate. Again, the purpose of these amendments was to permit financial aid to specified areas of the Commonwealth due to flooding and storms.

CONSTITUTIONAL CONVENTIONS

18. HOW MANY CONSTITUTIONS HAS PENNSYLVANIA HAD?

Four. The first Constitution was created in 1776 by a convention presided over by Benjamin Franklin. It was drafted when the great experiment of launching a free government in America was being undertaken and marked the passing of the old proprietary government and the transition from a colonial commonwealth.

The second Constitution, in 1790, eliminated features of the original document found to be unwise or unworkable. It gave the Commonwealth a body of law that served as a model for future state constitutions in Pennsylvania and many other states as well.

The convention that framed the Constitution of 1838 merely amended the previous version, keeping its main features intact.

The fourth Constitution, that of 1874, was largely a result of public demand to address the issue of special legislation. It was drafted and adopted to meet new conditions and problems that resulted from the rapid growth and development of the state during and following the Civil War.

19. HOW CAN THE CONSTITUTION BE REVISED?

It takes a constitutional convention, called for by law, enacted by the General Assembly and approved by the people.

20. SINCE THE PRESENT CONSTITUTION WAS ADOPTED, HOW MANY TIMES HAS THE QUESTION OF A CONSTITUTIONAL CONVENTION BEEN SUBMITTED TO THE PEOPLE?

Seven, most recently in the primary election of May 1967. The vote was 1,140,931 in favor of a constitutional convention and 703,576 against.

21. How many of those seven times was the question approved?

Only once, in 1967. That limited constitutional convention was called to consider the articles pertaining to legislative apportionment; judicial administration, organization, selection, and tenure; local government; taxation and state finance (with the exception of the uniformity clause already contained in the Constitution); and any amendment on the ballot in the 1967 primary election. As it turned out, the amendments on that ballot were approved, so they were not included at the convention.

Between 1873 and 1967, the question of a constitutional convention was defeated by the electorate six times.

22. By what vote were the four constitutions ratified?

The Constitution of 1776 was not submitted to the people for a vote, instead being adopted by the convention. Of 96 members, 95 were present when the Constitution was signed, but 23 failed to do so.

In 1790, the Constitution was again adopted by convention rather than submitted to the people. This time, of 69 members, 63 signed the document. The convention completed the new Constitution on February 6, 1790, and then recessed with the purpose of finding out how the people felt about it. They reassembled on September 2, 1790, for the signing and then adjourned.

The Constitution of 1838 was the first to be submitted to the people for ratification. The vote was 113,971 for and

112,759 against—a slim majority of 1,212 votes. The main support for this Constitution came from the northern and western counties, with opposition coming from southeastern counties and the large cities.

Pennsylvania's present Constitution was ratified by the people on December 16, 1873, by a vote of 253,744 for and 108,594 against.

23. **WHAT WERE THE EVENTS LEADING UP TO AND THE HIGHLIGHTS OF THE PENNSYLVANIA CONSTITUTIONAL CONVENTION OF 1967-68?**

Our present Constitution was drafted in 1872-73 and ratified in 1874. Even before the turn of the century, several of its provisions were outmoded, and they consequently hampered the government's ability to meet the people's changing needs. Nevertheless, voters rejected calls for open constitutional conventions six times between 1890 and 1963.

In 1967, the General Assembly passed, and the Governor approved, a bill calling for a limited constitutional convention to consider articles pertaining to: legislative apportionment; judicial administration, organization, selection and tenure; local government; taxation and state finance (except for the uniformity clause in the Constitution's taxation and finance article); and any amendment to the Constitution on the ballot in the 1967 primary election.

Because several of the originally proposed amendments were approved by the voters prior to the 1967 primary, only the four subject areas listed above needed to be addressed through a constitutional convention. The voters approved a limited convention to consider them in the 1967 primary election.

Act No. 2, the law authorizing the limited constitutional convention, called for the election of 150 delegates and designated 13 ex officio delegates, totalling 163. In the

November 1967 municipal election, voters elected three delegates from each of the state's 50 senatorial districts. The ex officio delegates included the Lieutenant Governor and the Majority and Minority leadership of both the Senate and the House.

Act No. 2 placed several restrictions on the convention. The Act:

- set a three-month life for the convention, from Dec. 1, 1967, to Feb. 29, 1968;

- prohibited the convention from making any recommendation permitting or prohibiting the imposition of a graduated income tax;

- prohibited changing the portion of the Constitution specifying that all taxes should be uniform, for the same class of subjects, within the territorial limits of the authority levying the tax; and

- prohibited the convention from altering the restriction that the Motor License Fund should be used solely for public highways, bridges, and air navigation facilities.

The Pennsylvania Constitutional Convention of 1967-68, convened in the Hall of the House of Representatives in Harrisburg, was organized by the following officers: Lt. Gov. Raymond J. Broderick, President of the convention; Robert P. Casey, First Vice President; Frank A. Orban, Jr., Second Vice President; and James A. Michener, Secretary.

During December, delegates submitted 209 proposals, which were referred to the appropriate committees and subcommittees where they were carefully studied, analyzed and discussed. Public hearings were then held to augment information gained from pre-convention hearings.

Seven proposals emerged through the subcommittee and public hearing review process. In February 1968, these proposals were given to the full convention for debate and amendment. They were adopted by the convention in early March and ratified by the voters on April 23, 1968.

"In all forms of government the people is the true legislator."

25

— Edmund Burke

The heart of Pennsylvania government is the General Assembly. These are the men and women elected by the people of the Commonwealth to serve as our state Senators and Representatives. As voters, we give them the right and responsibility to act on our behalf, expect them to be knowledgeable of the issues facing our citizens, and to do their best to lead us into the future.

The Pennsylvania Constitution, the laws of the state, and the customs of our government form an often stormy ocean across which our 253 legislators must navigate the ship of state.

This section provides an overview of the history of our state legislature, its structure, when and how it meets, who its officers are, and the mechanisms used to run our General Assembly.

The General Assembly is the branch of Pennsylvania government closest to the people. Each elected legislator represents, serves, and is responsible to a specific portion of the Commonwealth. It is up to the voters to determine how well they reflect the wants and needs of their constituencies and, through the election electoral process, whether or not they will be allowed to continue to serve.

STATE LEGISLATURES

24. *WHAT IS THE GENERAL ASSEMBLY?*

Pennsylvania's General Assembly is the legislative branch of government. Commonly called the state Legislature, it consists of two bodies—the Senate and the House of Representatives. The General Assembly's existence, authority, and limitations are provided by Article II of the Constitution.

25. *WHAT IS A UNICAMERAL LEGISLATURE?*

The word "cameral" comes from the Latin camera and the Greek kameral, both meaning "chamber." Therefore, a unicameral legislature consists of only one chamber or legislative house.

26. *WHAT IS A BICAMERAL LEGISLATURE?*

A bicameral legislature has two chambers or legislative houses.

Pennsylvania has had a bicameral legislature, consisting of the Senate and House of Representatives, since 1790. Prior to that date, Pennsylvania had a unicameral legislature with only the House of Representatives.

27. *HOW MANY STATES NOW HAVE A UNICAMERAL LEGISLATURE?*

One. Nebraska.

28. *WHAT STATE HAS THE LARGEST STATE LEGISLATURE?*

The New Hampshire Legislature includes 24 Senators and 400 state Representatives, for a total of 424.

29. *WHAT STATE HAS THE SMALLEST STATE LEGISLATURE?*

Alaska has the smallest bicameral legislature with 20 Senators and 40 state Representatives. Nebraska, however, has a smaller total representation (49) since there is only one chamber.

30. *HOW MANY MEMBERS ARE THERE IN THE PENNSYLVANIA LEGISLATURE?*

There are 253—50 Senators and 203 members of the House of Representatives.

31. *HAS IT ALWAYS HAD THIS NUMBER OF MEMBERS?*

No. In 1967, the Pennsylvania Constitution was amended to set the number of House members at 203.

When the House of Representatives first met in 1682, there were 42 members. By the early 1700s, that number dropped to 24 and then steadily increased to 76 by 1776.

In creating the Senate, the Pennsylvania Constitution of 1790 stipulated that this body should be no smaller than one-fourth of the House of Representatives and no larger than one-third, but it set no maximum for the House. When the House reached 100 members in 1855, a constitutional amendment in 1857 set that as the limit.

The Constitution of 1873 increased the Senate (then at 33 members) to 50 and set the House at a minimum of 200. Every county was guaranteed at least one member, regardless of its population.

The House peaked at 210 members for five sessions from 1955 until 1963. In order to adhere to the U.S. Supreme Court ruling of "one person, one vote," the Pennsylvania Constitution was amended to provide for 203 House members from districts "nearly equal in population." The first House to meet that standard convened in 1967.

LEGISLATIVE SESSIONS

32. WHAT IS A SESSION OF THE GENERAL ASSEMBLY?

A session of the General Assembly means that both the Senate and the House of Representatives are convened for the transaction of business.

33. HOW OFTEN DOES THE GENERAL ASSEMBLY MEET?

The General Assembly is a continuing body during the term for which its representatives are elected. It meets at noon on the first Tuesday of January and then regularly throughout the year.

34. IS THERE A LIMIT TO THE LENGTH OF A SESSION?

Yes, in a way. When the Constitution stipulates that the General Assembly must meet in regular session annually, that means the session of one year must adjourn by noon of the first Tuesday of the following year. Two regular sessions cannot meet at the same time.

The General Assembly must also adjourn by midnight, November 30, in even-numbered years due to the expiration of the terms of office of all House members and half the Senate.

Before 1960, the General Assembly met in regular session each odd-numbered year. The longest one was the 1955 session, which convened January 2, 1955, and adjourned May 22, 1956. During this 17-month period, the Assembly met in actual session on 168 days.

35. HOW MANY REGULAR SESSIONS HAVE THERE BEEN SINCE 1776?

The 178th regular session was convened on January 4, 1994. In the year 2000, the General Assembly will hold its 184th session.

36. **WHEN CAN THE GOVERNOR ADJOURN THE GENERAL ASSEMBLY?**

The Constitution allows the Governor to adjourn the General Assembly at "such times as he shall think proper, not exceeding four months," when the House and Senate disagree with respect to adjournment (see Article IV, Section 12).

No Governor has ever exercised this power, and many constitutional experts believe the provision only applies to special sessions.

37. **HOW CAN THE GOVERNOR CALL A SPECIAL SESSION OF THE GENERAL ASSEMBLY?**

Under the Constitution, the Governor can convene the General Assembly "on extraordinary occasions" by proclamation (see Article IV, Section 12).

The Governor can also call special sessions on petition of a majority of the members of both the House and Senate. The Senate can be convened by the Governor for the transaction of executive business.

38. **IS A SPECIAL SESSION OF THE GENERAL ASSEMBLY LIMITED IN ITS SUBJECT MATTER?**

Yes. When the General Assembly is convened in a special session, its members can only consider legislation on those subjects designated in the Governor's proclamation (see Article III, Section 12).

39. **HOW MANY SPECIAL SESSIONS OF THE GENERAL ASSEMBLY HAVE BEEN CALLED?**

There have been 34 special sessions.

At one point during the 1966 regular session, three special sessions ran concurrently. At that time, the regular session was limited only to fiscal matters, so in order to consider other legislation deemed to be of a general emergency nature, special sessions had to be called.

40. *CAN SESSIONS BE HELD ANYWHERE OTHER THAN THE SENATE AND HOUSE CHAMBERS?*

Yes, but the Constitution places two restrictions on this action (see Article II, Section 14). Sessions must be held in the City of Harrisburg, and if either body contemplates a move, it must have the consent of the other.

In case of enemy attack or other emergency, the Governor can declare an emergency temporary location.

41. *UNDER THE PRESENT CONSTITUTION, HAS THE LEGISLATURE EVER HELD SESSIONS ANYWHERE OTHER THAN THE CAPITOL?*

Yes. After the Main Capitol building burned on February 2, 1897, the Legislature met in the Grace Methodist Episcopal Church on State Street in Harrisburg for two years. In 1899, the Legislature temporarily moved to the Cobb Building, a large, square, brick warehouse built on the foundation of the destroyed Capitol. Because the Legislature felt that building was not adequate, $4 million was appropriated in 1899 for the construction of a new Capitol.

That Capitol, built around the Cobb Building, was completed in 1906 and dedicated by President Theodore Roosevelt on Oct. 4 of that year.

In 1987, a joint session was held in Philadelphia in honor of the bicentennial of the U.S. Constitution.

42. *CAN EITHER HOUSE ADJOURN FOR ANY LENGTH OF TIME WITHOUT THE CONSENT OF THE OTHER?*

The Constitution prohibits either body from adjourning for more than three days (Sundays excepted) without the consent of the other (see Article II, Section 14).

DISTRICT APPORTIONMENT

43. HOW ARE THE SENATORIAL AND REPRESENTATIVE DISTRICTS APPORTIONED?

The Constitution provides for the state to be divided into 50 senatorial districts and 203 representative districts. Each is to be composed of compact and contiguous territory as nearly equal in population as is practical. One Senator and one Representative are elected from each of the respective districts. No county, city, town, borough, township, or ward is to be divided in forming these districts unless absolutely necessary (see Article II, Section 16).

44. HOW OFTEN ARE THESE DISTRICTS REAPPORTIONED?

Every 10 years. A Legislative Reapportionment Commission, headed by a nonpartisan commissioner, conducts reapportionments in the year following each federal decennial census (see Article II, Section 17a). This provision was added to the Constitution by the limited Constitutional Convention of 1967-68. Prior to this, the General Assembly was required to do the reapportioning.

45. HOW DOES THE LEGISLATIVE REAPPORTION COMMISSION WORK?

The commission consists of five members, four of whom are the Majority and Minority leaders of both the Senate and the House of Representatives (or deputies appointed by each of them). Within 60 days after the official reporting of the federal decennial census, these four members must be certified by the President Pro Tempore of the Senate and the Speaker of the House of Representatives to the Secretary of the Commonwealth, who is the state's elections officer.

Within 45 days, these four members must select the fifth member, who serves as Chairman of the Commission. This person must be a citizen of the Commonwealth but cannot be a local, state, or federal official holding a paid office. If the four members fail to choose a chairman within that time, the state Supreme Court appoints the fifth member.

The commission has 90 days to file a preliminary reapportionment plan with the elections officer, and 30 days after the filing to make corrections to it.

Any person aggrieved by the preliminary plan has the same 30-day period to file exceptions with the commission. Then the commission has 30 days after the exception was filed to prepare a revised reapportionment plan. If no exceptions are filed, or if they are filed and acted upon, the commission's final plan becomes law.

Any aggrieved person can appeal the final plan directly to the state Supreme Court within 30 days. If it is established that the final plan is contrary to law, the court remands it to the commission for revision.

When the Supreme Court has finally decided an appeal, or when the last day for filing an appeal has passed with no appeal taken, the reapportionment plan has the force of law. The districts as outlined in the plan are then used in all elections to the General Assembly until the next reapportionment.

If the commission cannot meet the prescribed deadlines for filing its preliminary, revised, or final plan, the Supreme Court can extend the time periods if cause is shown. If no proper cause is shown, the court can immediately proceed to reapportion the Commonwealth on its own.

LEGISLATORS

Qualifications and Terms of Office

46. *WHAT IS A LEGISLATOR?*

A legislator is a member of the General Assembly. However, a member of the Senate is usually referred to as a Senator, and a member of the House of Representatives is referred to as a Representative.

47. *HOW ARE SENATORS AND REPRESENTATIVES ELECTED?*

They are chosen by popular vote of the people on the first Tuesday after the first Monday in November in every even-numbered year.

48. *HOW LONG ARE THEIR TERMS?*

Senators are elected for a term of four years and Representatives for a term of two years. All 203 members of the House and half of the Senate (25 members) are elected every two years (see Article II, Section 3).

49. *WHAT ARE THE QUALIFICATIONS NECESSARY TO BE ELECTED TO THE GENERAL ASSEMBLY?*

Senators must be at least 25 years old and Representatives at least 21 years old. They must be citizens and inhabitants of the state for four years, living in their respective districts for one year. They must reside within their district during their term of office (see Article II, Section 5).

50. *HOW IS A VACANCY FILLED IN THE EVENT OF THE DEATH OR RESIGNATION OF A MEMBER OF THE GENERAL ASSEMBLY?*

Whenever a vacancy occurs in the General Assembly, the presiding officer of the appropriate house issues a writ of election, setting a date for a special election within that district to fill the vacancy for the remainder of the term (see Article II, Section 2).

51. CAN A MEMBER OF THE GENERAL ASSEMBLY BE EXPELLED?

Yes. Either body can expel a member with a two-thirds vote. Anyone expelled for corruption can never run again for election to either house (see Article II, Section 11).

RESTRICTIONS

52. CAN A MEMBER OF THE GENERAL ASSEMBLY BE APPOINTED TO A CIVIL OFFICE?

No. During the term for which he or she is elected, no Senator or Representative can be appointed to any civil office under the Commonwealth, such as judge of the Court of Common Pleas, justice of the peace, member of the Turnpike Commission, or Public Utility Commission.

53. CAN A MEMBER OF THE GENERAL ASSEMBLY RESIGN THAT OFFICE IN ORDER TO BE APPOINTED TO A CIVIL OFFICE?

No. The Constitution prohibits such appointments for members of the General Assembly "during the time for which he is elected." Resignation cannot nullify constitutional intent and shorten the time during which a member is not eligible for appointment to civil office.

A Senator or Representative can, however, resign his or her office in order to be elected by the people to another office.

54. **CAN A MEMBER OF CONGRESS SERVE AT THE SAME TIME IN THE GENERAL ASSEMBLY?**

No. This is specifically prohibited by the Constitution (see Article II, Section 6).

55. **WHAT CRIMES DISQUALIFY A PERSON FROM BEING ELECTED TO THE GENERAL ASSEMBLY?**

No person can be elected to the General Assembly who has been convicted of:

- embezzlement of public monies (intentional and fraudulent taking of money or property entrusted to one's care for private or personal use);

- bribery (giving or receiving money, anything of value, or any valuable service intended to influence a person's discharge of a legal duty);

- perjury (making a false statement, verbally or in writing, while under oath); or

- other infamous crimes (one that would render a person incompetent as a witness or juror) (see Article II, Section 7).

These crimes would also disqualify a person from holding any office of trust or profit in the Commonwealth.

In addition, any member expelled from the General Assembly is prohibited from future election to either house.

56. **WHEN IS A MEMBER EXCUSED OR BARRED FROM VOTING IN THE GENERAL ASSEMBLY?**

According to the Constitution, a legislator may not vote on any bill or measure in which he or she has a private or personal interest (see Article III, Section 13).

While the Constitution does not spell out what a private or personal interest might be, this section was added to the document at a time when members were representing corporations seeking special legislation and special favors.

Over the years, presiding officers have held that the right to represent one's constituency is of major importance, and a legislator should not be barred or excused from voting on matters of direct personal interest except in clear cases. It must be a situation that affects the legislator individually and not as a member of a certain class or profession.

SENIORITY

57. *DO MEMBERS HAVE INDIVIDUAL SEATS ASSIGNED TO THEM?*

Yes. Seats in the Senate are assigned by the President Pro Tempore, usually according to seniority. Democrats sit on the west side of the chamber, to the President's right; Republicans sit on the left or east side of the chamber. In the House, seating is also by seniority, with Democrats to the right of the Speaker and Republicans to the left.

58. *WHAT IS MEANT BY "SENIORITY RULE"?*

It is customary that the member who has served longest on the majority side of a committee becomes chairman of that committee and also acquires additional influence.

OFFICERS AND KEY EMPLOYEES

59. *WHO ARE THE PRINCIPAL OFFICERS OF THE SENATE AND HOW ARE THEY CHOSEN?*

The principal officers are the President Pro Tempore, the Secretary, and the Chief Clerk, and all are elected by the Senate. As a constitutional officer, the President Pro Tempore is the only one who is also a Senator. The Secretary and Chief Clerk are statutory officers.

60. *WHO PRESIDES OVER THE SENATE?*

The Lieutenant Governor is President of the Senate by authority of the Constitution (see Article IV, Section 4).

The Senate elects from its members a President Pro Tempore to preside in the absence of the President. If both the President and the President Pro Tempore are absent, then the Majority Leader, or someone designated by the Majority Leader, presides. When this happens, the Majority Leader is vested with all the powers of the President (except as specifically prohibited by the Constitution or laws). This authority, however, does not extend beyond the day's adjournment.

61. *WHAT ARE THE DUTIES OF THE LIEUTENANT GOVERNOR WHILE PRESIDING OVER THE SENATE?*

The President of the Senate takes the chair each day and calls the Senate to order. The President's duties include referring bills to committees, preserving order, preventing personal reflections, confining members in debate to the question at hand, and stating all questions. The President signs all bills and joint resolutions passed by both houses as well as all orders, addresses, writs, warrants, and subpoenas.

62. *CAN THE LIEUTENANT GOVERNOR VOTE IN THE SENATE?*

The Lieutenant Governor, as President of the Senate, can cast a tie-breaking vote on any question except the final passage of a bill or joint resolution, the adoption of a conference report, or the concurrence in amendments made by the House of Representatives (see Article IV, Section 4).

63. *HAS A PRESIDENT OF THE SENATE EVER RESIGNED?*

Yes. John C. Bell resigned on January 2, 1947, 20 days before the expiration of his term, in order to become Governor. He replaced Governor Edward Martin, who was elected to the United States Senate.

64. *WHAT ARE THE DUTIES OF THE PRESIDENT PRO TEMPORE?*

The Constitution provides for the President Pro Tempore to perform the duties of the President of the Senate (Lieutenant Governor) in case of the President's absence or disability. Senate rules allow the President Pro Tempore to exercise all powers and duties of the President.

In addition, he appoints the chairmen, vice chairmen, and members of the committees, both standing and special.

65. *DOES THE PRESIDENT PRO TEMPORE OF THE SENATE VOTE?*

Yes. As a member of the Senate, the President Pro Tempore participates in debates and votes.

66. *WHO ARE THE PRINCIPAL OFFICERS OF THE HOUSE OF REPRESENTATIVES?*

The principal officers in the House are the Speaker, the Chief Clerk, the Parliamentarian, and the Comptroller. Except for the Parliamentarian, all are elected by the House, but the Speaker is the only officer who is a member of that body.

67. *WHO PRESIDES OVER THE HOUSE OF REPRESENTATIVES?*

The presiding officer is the Speaker of the House, who is nominated at a party caucus and chosen by a majority vote of the members of the House of Representatives. The Speaker may appoint a Speaker Pro Tempore.

68. *WHAT ARE THE DUTIES OF THE SPEAKER?*

- Presiding over the House of Representatives;
- Preserving order and decorum; deciding all questions of order;
- Signing all bills and joint resolutions passed by both houses;
- Referring all bills and resolutions to committees;
- Appointing the chairmen and vice chairmen of the standing committees;
- Appointing all special or select committees; and
- Voting on all questions.

69. *COULD A PERSON OTHER THAN AN ELECTED REPRESENTATIVE SERVE AS THE SPEAKER?*

No. The Constitution requires that the House select one of its members as Speaker (see Article II, Section 9).

70. *WHAT IS A PARTY LEADER?*

In debate, members do not refer to Democrats and Republicans but to the "Majority" and the "Minority," each of which has a leader. The party leaders head the debate and bring forward their respective party's programs or policies. The leader's advocacy of or opposition to proposed legislation indicates the party's stand.

The Majority Leader has enormous control over which legislative programs are discussed and when.

71. *DOES THE GENERAL ASSEMBLY ELECT THE MAJORITY AND MINORITY LEADERS?*

No. The Majority and Minority leaders of the Senate and House are not officers, and are therefore not elected by the membership. The leaders are chosen by party caucuses.

72. WHAT ARE THE DUTIES OF THE SENATE AND HOUSE "WHIPS"?

Like most of our parliamentary procedures, party "Whips" originated in the British Parliament. For important debates, kings and ministers made a great effort to bring their followers together; this was referred to as "whipping them in." An individual heading such an effort was known as a "whipper in," eventually shortened to "whip."

Today, Whips are the eyes and ears of their respective party's floor leaders, and it is their job to discern the direction in which opinions are moving and to appease any mutterings or discontent. Through the Whips, the party system is used to conduct the business of the Senate and House.

A Whip's most important task is to gather and hold together the members of a party for united action when important votes are to be taken.

73. HOW ARE ADMINISTRATIVE AND FINANCIAL POLICIES SET IN THE GENERAL ASSEMBLY?

In the House of Representatives, financial rules are established by a majority vote of the members. Specific policies are dictated by the Committee on Rules and the Bipartisan Management Committee (BMC).

The BMC is responsible for implementation of these policies as well as the administrative functions of the House. This includes oversight of the Office of the Chief Clerk (responsible for day-to-day operations of the House) and the Office of the Comptroller (responsible for the fiscal affairs of the House). Facilities, resources, and services provided by the Chief Clerk and the Comptroller are provided to all members and staff on an impartial basis.

The BMC consists of five members: the Speaker, the Majority Leader and Whip, and the Minority Leader and Whip. All actions of the BMC require the vote of at least four of the five members.

Like the House, the financial rules of the Senate are established by a majority vote of its members. Specific policies are established by the Committee on Management Operations, which is responsible for the Senate's administrative and financial functions.

The Committee on Management Operations oversees the Office of the Secretary (responsible for day-to-day operations of the Senate) and the Office of the Chief Clerk (responsible for the Senate's financial affairs).

The seven-member committee includes the President Pro Tempore and the Majority and Minority Leaders, Whips, and Appropriations Committee chairmen.

74.   WHAT ARE THE DUTIES OF THE PARLIAMENTARIAN?

The Parliamentarian assists in rendering correct parliamentary decisions and in ensuring that the practices and precedents of the House are conducted according to law. This officer must be well-versed in the rules and precedents of the House in order to render sound decisions at a moment's notice.

COMMITTEES

Standing Committees

75.   WHY ARE STANDING COMMITTEES NECESSARY?

Standing committees, as permanent units of the General Assembly, serve as the workshops of the Legislature. It is their duty to carefully study all bills referred to them and to prepare bills to be reported with a favorable recommendation to each house.

The Constitution requires that "no bill shall be considered unless referred to a committee" (see Article III, Section 2).

During an average session, more than 4,000 bills, representing a wide range of subjects, are introduced in both houses. Many of these bills are controversial and require long debate and consideration of many amendments. Without an effective committee system, it would be impossible for the General Assembly to attend to its business of enacting new laws, amending present ones, appropriating money, investigating governmental operations, and seeing to other duties.

76. HOW ARE THE MEMBERS OF THE STANDING COMMITTEES SELECTED?

In the Senate, the chairmen, vice chairmen and committee members are chosen by the President Pro Tempore. Each Senator completes a form to indicate committee preferences, and that information is taken into consideration by that official when making committee assignments.

In the House, a Committee on Committees (consisting of the Speaker, 10 Majority members, and five Minority members) recommends to the House the names of the members of the committees. Chairmen and vice chairmen are appointed by the Speaker.

These procedures are provided for in Senate and House rules.

77. **Do standing committees hold public hearings on all bills?**

No. Each committee decides whether or not to hold hearings on any particular legislation.

78. **Are committee meetings open to the public?**

Yes. The "Sunshine Act" (Act 84 of 1986) makes all committee meetings in which bills are considered or testimony taken open to the public. This does not apply to party caucuses or any Senate or House Ethics Committee.

79. **Does a standing committee control the disposition of the bills that are referred to it?**

Yes. Ordinarily, a committee's failure to act on a measure spells its defeat.

80. **Can a committee be discharged from consideration of a bill?**

Yes. There are provisions in the rules of both the Senate and the House to discharge a committee.

In the Senate, a measure can be discharged from consideration within 10 legislative days of its referral only with unanimous consent of the full Senate. After 10 legislative days, it can be discharged by a majority vote of the members.

In the House, a bill cannot be discharged until 15 legislative days after its referral. A resolution to discharge a measure must be passed by a majority vote of the House members.

81. **Are committee records and files open to the public?**

Yes. The proceedings of all committee meetings and records of votes taken on any measure are open to the public.

Other Committees

82. *WHAT IS A SELECT COMMITTEE?*

A select committee is established by the Senate or the House for a special purpose and for a limited time. When the select committee's function has been carried out and a report made, it is automatically dissolved.

83. *WHAT IS A CONFERENCE COMMITTEE?*

Differences of opinion over legislation between the two houses of the General Assembly are committed to conference committees for settlement. This usually happens when a bill passes one house with amendments that are unacceptable to the other house.

The house that disagrees with the amendments will ask for a conference, and the presiding officer then appoints the conference members, or "managers." Three members of the House and three from the Senate are named to the committee—two from the majority party and one from the minority. After deliberation, an identical report is signed by at least two of the committee members from each house and must be accepted or rejected as a whole by both chambers.

If accepted by both houses, the bill is signed by the presiding officers and sent to the Governor. Sometimes, however, the conference committee fails to reach an agreement. Unless all differences are finally adjusted, the bill fails.

84. *WHAT IS A COMMITTEE OF THE WHOLE?*

A committee of the whole is the entire membership of the Senate or House sitting as a committee. Its purpose is to permit more informal debate than could be held under ordinary restricted rules of procedure. The presiding officer appoints some other member to preside over a committee of the whole.

This procedure has been very rarely used in the Pennsylvania General Assembly.

LEGISLATIVE PROCESS

Rules of Procedure

85. *How are the rules of procedure in the General Assembly determined?*

The Constitution provides that "each house shall have power to determine the rules of its proceedings" (see Article II, Section 11).

The parliamentary practices of the Senate and House come from six sources:

- the Pennsylvania Constitution,

- statutory law,

- rules adopted by the Senate and House,

- precedents established by the presiding officers of each house,

- *Jefferson's Manual*, which lists the rules and precedents of the U.S. House of Representatives, and

- *Mason's Manual*, containing the rules of procedure for legislative bodies.

86. *What is a caucus?*

The word "caucus" is a political term denoting a special form of party meeting. It originated in Boston in the early 18th century. At that time, it meant a political club where public matters were discussed, arrangements were made for local elections, and candidates for office were chosen.

Today, a caucus is a meeting of the members of a political party in the U.S. Congress or a state legislature in which party policy on proposed legislation is discussed and refined.

87. WHAT IS A QUORUM?

A quorum is a majority of those members elected, sworn, and living, whose membership has not been terminated by resignation or action of the body.

88. HOW DOES A MEMBER OF THE GENERAL ASSEMBLY OBTAIN PERMISSION TO SPEAK?

When a Senator wishes to speak, he or she rises, addresses the presiding officer, and may not proceed until recognized.

When a Representative wishes to speak, he or she addresses the Speaker and may continue when recognized.

89. ARE THERE ANY RESTRICTIONS ON DEBATE?

Debate must be confined to the question under consideration. Statements on other subjects can only be made by unanimous consent of the body. Members may not speak more than twice on any question without the consent of the chamber. There is no time constraint unless there has been an agreement to limit debate. Debate can be terminated by a motion for the previous question.

90. WHAT IS THE "PREVIOUS QUESTION"?

A motion for the previous question, if agreed to by a majority of the members present, cuts off all debate and brings the body to direct vote on the immediate question.

In the Senate, the motion must be made by not less than four members. In the House, the motion must be made and seconded by 20 members.

91. WHAT IS A FILIBUSTER?

The word "filibuster" originally meant a buccaneer (such as those who plundered the Spanish colonies in America) and later, military adventurers who led private armed expeditions into foreign countries.

From this general idea, the term has come to be used to refer to organized obstructive tactics in legislative bodies. It is the practice of deliberately taking advantage of the freedom of debate in order to delay or prevent action on a measure.

The call for the previous question virtually eliminates the chance of a filibuster in the Pennsylvania General Assembly.

92. WHAT BUSINESS CAN BE TRANSACTED BY UNANIMOUS CONSENT?

Practically anything can be done in either the Senate or the House by unanimous consent, except when the Constitution specifically prohibits it. For example, the Constitution requires a roll call vote for the final passage of a bill, so the presiding officer cannot consider a unanimous consent request to waive this requirement.

Objection by one member defeats a request for unanimous consent.

93. ARE VISITORS ALLOWED TO OBSERVE THE PROCEEDINGS IN THE GENERAL ASSEMBLY?

Yes. Both houses have visitors' galleries. Visitors are subject to control by the presiding officers, and the galleries can be cleared if there is disorder. The Constitution provides for closing sessions to the public if the business is such as should be kept secret (see Article II, Section 13).

94. *WHAT PROVISIONS ARE MADE FOR MEMBERS OF THE MEDIA COVERING THE PROCEEDINGS OF THE GENERAL ASSEMBLY?*

Special spaces are set aside in each house for accredited representatives of the print and broadcast media. There is also a newsroom in the Capitol for use by members of the media.

95. *WHAT IS THE SIGNIFICANCE OF THE MACE?*

The history of the mace goes back to early Roman times. It consisted of a bundle of birch or elm rods bound together by a red thong with an ax blade protruding from the top of the bundle. Officers carried it in advance of magistrates and emperors to show authority. Occasionally the mace was used to flog or to execute condemned Roman citizens.

In medieval times, the mace became an offensive weapon made of iron or steel. It could break through the strongest armor and was carried in battle by bishops to adhere to the church canon forbidding priests to shed blood.

Purely ceremonial maces were first used in the 12th century during the reigns of Philip II of France and Richard I of England. They were carried by a royal bodyguard called a sergeant at arms. Today's ceremonial maces are used by legislative assemblies as a symbol of authority, reminding the members of the power of the assembly to preserve order and dignity.

The maces used by the Pennsylvania Senate and House of Representatives are almost identical, with a slight variation in size. Both are of solid mahogany topped by a brass sphere engraved with the coat of arms of the Commonwealth on each side.

In the Senate, the mace is placed on the rostrum behind the President and to his right on the opening day of the session and remains there until final adjournment. The mace is only removed during session to escort the President and members of the Senate to the House of Representatives for a joint session or to lead a delegation of members to funeral services for a fellow Senator or former Senator. The sergeant at arms has full custody of and responsibility for the mace.

In the House of Representatives, the mace is carried by the sergeant at arms escorting the Speaker into the chamber to open each session day. It then remains in a pedestal to the right of the Speaker's desk until recess or adjournment.

Aside from preserving peace and order, the mace demonstrates the Legislature's respect for its own heritage and law. It symbolizes the guarantee that those who govern are also governed.

Bills, Acts, and Resolutions

96. **WHAT IS THE DIFFERENCE BETWEEN A BILL AND AN ACT?**

A "bill" is the constitutional designation of a proposed law introduced into either house (see Article III, Section 1).

The term "act" refers to a bill that has been passed by both houses and becomes law, whether by approval of the Governor, lack of action by the Governor in the time allotted by the Constitution, or by passage over the Governor's veto by a two-thirds vote of both houses (see question #111).

97. WHAT IS A CALENDAR OF BILLS?

A calendar of bills, or legislative calendar, is a daily work sheet of those measures reported from committees and ready for consideration by the Senate and the House.

98. WHAT IS MEANT BY "CONSIDERING" A BILL?

The Pennsylvania Constitution requires that each bill be considered on three different days in both the Senate and the House (see Article III, Section 4). When a bill is reported from committee to the full House or Senate, it is given a first consideration, and if amended, is reprinted to show any changes made by the committee.

After agreeing to the bill on first consideration, it is advanced without debate to the calendar of bills on second consideration, where it may be amended further.

99. WHY MUST TAX BILLS ORIGINATE IN THE HOUSE OF REPRESENTATIVES?

The constitutional provision stating that "all bills for raising revenue shall originate in the House of Representatives" is an adaptation of the English practice (see Article III, Section 10). The principle is to make the purse strings controlled by the body closest to the people.

This section of the Pennsylvania Constitution was taken from an almost identical provision in the U.S. Constitution written when U.S. Senators were chosen by the state legislatures.

100. CAN THE SENATE AMEND TAX BILLS?

Yes. The Constitution says that "the Senate may propose amendments as in other bills" (see Article III, Section 10).

101. WHAT RESTRICTIONS ARE PLACED ON ITEMS CONTAINED IN THE GENERAL APPROPRIATION BILL?

The Constitution says that the general appropriation bill can only authorize funds for the ordinary expenses of the executive, legislative, and judicial departments; for interest on the public debt; and for public schools (see Article III, Section 11). All other appropriations, which are the legislative authorizations necessary to allow an expenditure of state government funds, must be made by separate bill, each covering only one subject.

This section was added to the Constitution to end the practice of putting an unpopular measure into the general appropriation bill in order to compel members to vote for it rather than defeat the general bill.

102. WHAT VOTE IS REQUIRED TO PASS BILLS APPROPRIATING MONEY TO CHARITABLE AND EDUCATIONAL INSTITUTIONS?

A vote of two-thirds of the members in each house is necessary for an appropriation to be made to any charitable or educational institution not under the absolute control of the Commonwealth (see Article III, Section 30).

This is known as a "non-preferred" appropriation.

103. WHAT APPROPRIATIONS ARE FORBIDDEN?

The Constitution forbids appropriations to any person or community for charitable, educational, or benevolent purposes or to any denominational or sectarian institution, corporation, or association (see Article III, Section 29).

104. WHAT IS A DEFICIENCY BILL?

A deficiency bill authorizes funds to supplement insufficient appropriations. Appropriations are normally made in advance of a fiscal year on the basis of estimates for that year. However, conditions may arise that exhaust the appropriation before the end of that time.

105. WHAT IS A RESOLUTION?

A resolution is a form of written proposal used to make declarations, state policies, or announce decisions when some other form of legislative action is not required. For example, a statute, or law, cannot be enacted by resolution.

Resolutions can be recognized by the use of the word "resolved" in its acting or declaratory clause.

106. HOW MANY KINDS OF RESOLUTIONS ARE THERE?

There are three kinds of resolutions that can be acted upon by the General Assembly. A simple resolution is passed by one house only. A concurrent resolution must pass both houses, and if it commits the state to action, it must be sent to the Governor for consideration. A joint resolution, which usually proposes an amendment to the Constitution, requires action by both houses but is not sent to the Governor.

107. HOW ARE VOTES TAKEN IN THE GENERAL ASSEMBLY?

Votes are taken two ways—voice and roll call. On a voice vote, the presiding officer of either house asks all those in favor to say "aye" and those opposed to say "no."

On a roll call vote in the Senate, the name of each member is called in alphabetical order. Each member responds either "aye" or "no," and the clerks record the vote accordingly.

In the House of Representatives, the roll call vote is taken electronically. The speaker unlocks the voting system and each member votes by moving a switch on his or her desk. The vote is recorded beside the members' names on a large, lighted board—a green light for "aye" and red for "no." A running total is kept of the votes being cast, and then the board displays the final vote. When the speaker determines that all members present have voted, the results are recorded on a special roll call sheet.

108. WHAT IS A CONSTITUTIONAL MAJORITY?

A constitutional majority is the number of affirmative votes required by the Constitution for a body to take a particular action. For example, to pass legislation in the General Assembly, a majority of the members elected is required.

In the Senate, with 50 members, 26 votes are a constitutional majority. When a two-thirds vote is required, 34 votes are needed.

In the House of Representatives, with 203 members, 102 votes make up a constitutional majority, and 136 are needed for a two-thirds vote.

109. WHAT IS A SIMPLE MAJORITY?

A simple majority requires a quorum to be present and is a majority of that group (see question #87). A simple majority is enough to carry any proposition unless otherwise specified by Constitution, statute, or rule.

Therefore, the smallest legal vote in the Senate could be 14 to 12; while the smallest vote in the House could be 52 to 50.

Voting

110. CAN ANY VOTE BY THE GENERAL ASSEMBLY BE RECONSIDERED?

The General Assembly does have the inherent right to reconsider its vote on an action, with certain exceptions.

An action cannot be reconsidered when it is not possible to cancel, nullify, or void its effects. In general, an action cannot be cancelled when vested rights have been acquired as a result of it (as in a contract); when rights cannot be legally or constitutionally taken away; or when the subject is beyond the control or out of reach of the body.

A motion to reconsider an action must be made on the same day it was originally taken or within the next five session days.

Actions Open to the Governor

111. **WHAT HAPPENS WHEN A BILL IS PRESENTED TO THE GOVERNOR FOR SIGNING?**

When a bill is sent to the Governor, one of four things can happen:

a) The Governor can sign it, whereupon it becomes a law.

b) The Governor can veto the bill. In this case, the General Assembly can choose to vote on it again. A two-thirds vote of all members in both houses will override the veto.

c) The Governor can hold it for a time without taking action—either signature or veto—(10 days while the General Assembly is in session or 30 days after final adjournment), after which it will automatically become law. The Governor's refusal to sign a bill may indicate disapproval of the measure but with an acknowledgement that a veto is either useless or politically unwise. It may also indicate that the Governor is undecided about the bill's constitutionality.

d) The Governor can employ a line-item veto. This means that any portion of a bill that appropriates money for a particular use can be disapproved while allowing for remaining parts of the bill to become law. Those items vetoed by the Governor can still be restored by a legislative override.

112. WHAT IS A VETO?

The word "veto" is a Latin verb that means "I forbid."

The Governor has the constitutional right to refuse to approve any measure passed by the General Assembly, and in such cases, returns it to the house of origin with a statement of objections. A veto applies to an entire measure, except for line-item vetoes of appropriations bills (see question #111).

113. CAN THE GOVERNOR VETO A RESOLUTION PROPOSING A CONSTITUTIONAL AMENDMENT?

No. The Governor does not have the chance to either approve or veto such a resolution. Since it is not a bill enacting a law, it is not presented to the Governor for consideration.

A resolution proposing a constitutional amendment, after passage in both houses, is filed with the Secretary of the Commonwealth for submission to a vote of the people at the proper time (see question #15).

114. IS THERE EVER A CEREMONY WHEN THE GOVERNOR SIGNS A BILL INTO LAW?

Usually the Governor signs bills without any particular fanfare. On occasion, when a bill is of special public significance, a ceremony for the signing will be held. Sometimes more than one pen will be used by the Governor to sign a bill, and these are given to the individuals most interested in the legislation.

115. *WHAT HAPPENS TO A BILL AFTER IT IS SIGNED BY THE GOVERNOR?*

The signed bill is sent to the Secretary of the Commonwealth where it is given an act number and becomes known as a statute. The Secretary notifies the director of the Legislative Reference Bureau, who has all statutes printed and indexed in a bound volume called *Laws of Pennsylvania.*

IMPEACHMENT

116. *WHAT IS IMPEACHMENT?*

A proceeding brought against a public official by the General Assembly seeking that official's removal from public office due to misbehavior in office.

117. *WHO HAS THE POWER OF IMPEACHMENT?*

The Constitution gives sole power to initiate the impeachment process to the House of Representatives (see Article VI, Section 4).

118. *WHO CONDUCTS IMPEACHMENT TRIALS?*

The Constitution requires all impeachments to be tried by the Senate (see Article VI, Section 5).

119. *WHAT VOTE IS NEEDED FOR IMPEACHMENT?*

No one can be convicted in an impeachment trial without a two-thirds vote of the Senate members present.

120. *WHO CAN BE IMPEACHED?*

According to the Constitution, the Governor and all other civil officers are liable for impeachment for any misbehavior in office (see Article VI, Section 6).

121. WHAT IS THE HISTORY OF IMPEACHMENT IN THE PENNSYLVANIA GENERAL ASSEMBLY?

Pennsylvania has not often used the impeachment process, probably because citizens are wary of political trials. The House of Representatives demands very clear and serious evidence before it will begin the impeachment process.

The first impeachment was in 1685, barely three years after the founding of the unicameral Colonial House. Nicholas More, a physician and the second Speaker of the House, was expelled from the body and removed by the Governor as judge of the Provincial Court.

In 1803, the House impeached three Pennsylvania Supreme Court judges, but the Senate acquitted them.

On three different occasions in 1816, the House voted to impeach Judge Walter Franklin. But his attorney, James Buchanan, (only 25 and just completing two years as a Representative) argued brilliantly to convince the General Assembly that it should undertake impeachment only in the most dire circumstances. Buchanan later became the 15th President of the United States.

Efforts were made to impeach Governor George H. Earle during the Great Depression of the 1930s for failing to send the state police to arrest unemployed bootleg coal miners in northeastern Pennsylvania. The House, however, did not consider the charge serious enough.

On May 24, 1994, Rolf Larsen, Justice of the Supreme Court of Pennsylvania, was impeached by the House. As of the printing of this book, he was awaiting trial in the Senate.

LOBBYING

122. *WHAT IS LOBBYING?*

Lobbying is a long-standing practice in all legislative bodies whereby both private and public groups attempt to influence government policy.

123. *WHAT IS A LOBBYIST?*

A lobbyist is someone who tries to influence the voting of legislators, often on behalf of a group of like-minded individuals or organizations. Since much of this work is done by personal contact, and since legislators may not be approached on the floor of either chamber while in session, the contact is often made in the offices and lobbies of the Senate and House.

Lobbyists who are compensated for their services must register with the Secretary of the Senate and Chief Clerk of the House of Representatives.

124. *HOW DOES LOBBYING BENEFIT THE LEGISLATURE?*

Lobbying plays a vital role in our form of government. The complexities of modern life are evidenced by the large number of bills brought before the Legislature each session. It is impossible for legislators to know the problems confronting all the various groups representing the citizens of the state.

Members often confer with lobbyists for information and technical details concerning the potential effects of pending legislation. It is of great value to get the point of view of a farmers' or bankers' association, a labor union, senior citizens, or any other group concerned with relevant legislation.

The executive branch of Pennsylvania government, consisting of both elected and appointed officials, is headed by the Governor, who holds the state's highest office. Citizens look to the Governor as a leader who will set the agenda for state government, see that current problems are dealt with effectively and that plans for the future are put into place.

The Attorney General, Auditor General, and State Treasurer, all of whom are elected to administer agencies independent of the Governor, are also executive-branch officials. The Lieutenant Governor, an elected official, and the appointed members of the Governor's cabinet constitute the rest of the executive branch of government. Cabinet members manage the operations of state government agencies and provide their expertise as advisors to the Governor.

This section includes a description of some of the duties and powers of Pennsylvania's Governor as well as information about other state executive officers.

125. WHAT IS THE EXECUTIVE DEPARTMENT?

The Pennsylvania Constitution defines the executive department as consisting of the Governor, Lieutenant Governor, Attorney General, Auditor General, State Treasurer, and Secretary of Education (see Article IV, Section 1). The executive department, however, has grown to include all state government agencies under the jurisdiction of the Governor.

126. WHO HAS EXECUTIVE POWER?

The Constitution grants supreme executive power to the Governor (see Article IV, Section 2).

The Constitution of 1776 gave executive power to a Supreme Executive Council composed of 12 members elected by the House every three years. The Governor has had supreme executive power in Pennsylvania since the Constitution of 1790.

127. WHAT IS THE OATH OF OFFICE TAKEN BY THE GOVERNOR?

The Governor takes the same oath of office as do all members of the General Assembly and all judicial, state, and county officers. The wording of that oath is as follows:

"I do solemnly swear (or affirm*) that I will support, obey and defend the Constitution of the United States and the Constitution of this Commonwealth and that I will discharge the duties of my office with fidelity."

* **NOTE:** If the individual taking the oath objects to the term "swear," which is a declaration that implies an appeal to God, that individual may substitute the word "affirm."

128. WHERE IS THE INAUGURATION CEREMONY FOR THE GOVERNOR-ELECT HELD?

The Governor-elect can choose the site, but the ceremony must be held in Harrisburg. It usually takes place on the front steps of the Main Capitol Building.

129. WHO ADMINISTERS THE OATH OF OFFICE?

The oath of office is administered to the Governor-elect by the Chief Justice of the Pennsylvania Supreme Court.

130. ON WHAT DATE DOES A GOVERNOR'S TERM BEGIN?

The Constitution says that the Governor's term will begin at noon on the third Tuesday of January following the election (see Article IV, Section 3).

131. HOW IS THE LIEUTENANT GOVERNOR ELECTED?

The Constitution provides for the Lieutenant Governor to be elected jointly with the Governor (see Article IV, Section 4).

The Constitution of 1874 called for the Lieutenant Governor to be "chosen at the same time, in the same manner, for the same term and subject to the same provisions as the Governor." Each, however, was voted on separately.

An amendment to the Constitution in 1967 set today's system of a gubernatorial candidate running with a candidate for Lieutenant Governor. The President and Vice President of the United States are elected in this same manner.

132. CAN A GOVERNOR HOLD OFFICE FOR MORE THAN ONE TERM?

Yes, since 1967, the Constitution limits a Governor to two consecutive terms of four years each (see Article IV, Section 3).

In 1967, the voters approved the amendment to the Constitution that allows the Governor to serve two terms. Previously, the Governor was not eligible to serve two successive terms.

133. WHAT HAPPENS IF THE GOVERNOR DIES, RESIGNS, BECOMES DISABLED, OR IS REMOVED FROM OFFICE?

If the Governor cannot fulfill the duties of office for any of these reasons, the Constitution grants executive power to the Lieutenant Governor (see Article IV, Section 13).

In 1974, the General Assembly enacted a law providing the procedure for determining the disability of the Governor and Lieutenant Governor, and the succession in accordance with the Constitution.

134. WHAT PROVISIONS ARE THERE FOR THE CONTINUATION OF GOVERNMENT IN THE EVENT OF AN ATTACK ON THE UNITED STATES OR OTHER EMERGENCY?

The Emergency Interim Executive and Judicial Succession Act of 1959 provides for continuity of government in the event of an attack on the United States. It states that if the Governor, Lieutenant Governor and President Pro Tempore of the Senate are all unable or unavailable to exercise executive power, the Speaker of the House is next in line to discharge the duties of the Governor.

The Speaker would only hold power until a new Governor was elected or until one of the preceding officers became available.

135. FOR HOW LONG CAN THIS AUTHORITY BE EXERCISED?

The Legislature, by concurrent resolution, can at any time terminate the authority of any official authorized to act as Governor following an attack on the United States.

136. DURING AN ATTACK, CAN THE SEAT OF GOVERNMENT BE MOVED FROM HARRISBURG?

Yes. Whether due to the effects of an enemy attack or the anticipated effects of a threatened attack, the Governor can, by proclamation, declare an emergency temporary location for the seat of government.

137. IF THE LIEUTENANT GOVERNOR BECOMES GOVERNOR, WHO TAKES OVER AS LIEUTENANT GOVERNOR?

The President Pro Tempore of the Senate would become Lieutenant Governor and could then become Governor if another vacancy should occur. If the President Pro Tempore should become Governor, that seat in the Senate would become vacant and would be filled by election as any other Senate vacancy.

138. WHO BECOMES GOVERNOR IF THE GOVERNOR-ELECT DIES OR IS DISQUALIFIED BEFORE TAKING THE OATH OF OFFICE?

The Lieutenant Governor.

139. WHAT IF BOTH THE GOVERNOR-ELECT AND THE LIEUTENANT GOVERNOR-ELECT DIE OR ARE DISQUALIFIED BEFORE INAUGURATION?

In that case, the President Pro Tempore of the Senate would assume the governorship.

140. WHO WAS THE FIRST GUBERNATORIAL CANDIDATE TO BE CHOSEN BY A PARTY NOMINATING CONVENTION?

In 1820, William Findlay, a Democrat from Franklin County, was nominated for Governor by a convention of delegates chosen by the Democrats for this special purpose. Earlier candidates were chosen by legislative caucuses.

Used for the first time in Pennsylvania, this method of nominating candidates soon spread to other states and is now used by the national parties for choosing presidential candidates.

141. WHO WAS THE YOUNGEST GOVERNOR OF PENNSYLVANIA? THE OLDEST?

Robert Pattison was the youngest Governor. He was 32 years old at the time he was elected. Governor Pattison served two terms, 1883-87 and 1891-95.

At 69, David Lawrence was Pennsylvania's oldest Governor. He took the oath of office in 1959 and served until his term expired in January 1963.

142. WHO ARE THE ELECTED OFFICERS OF THE COMMONWEALTH?

The Governor, Lieutenant Governor, Treasurer, Auditor General, and Attorney General are Pennsylvania's elected officers.

143. WHAT ARE THE TERMS OF OFFICE OF THE ATTORNEY GENERAL, AUDITOR GENERAL, AND STATE TREASURER?

Their terms are four years, beginning on the third Tuesday of January following their election.

144. ARE THEIR TERMS LIMITED?

Yes. They are not allowed to serve for more than two successive terms.

145. WHO ARE MEMBERS OF THE GOVERNOR'S CABINET?

The Governor's cabinet includes, in the order of creation: the Secretary of the Commonwealth (established in 1777); Adjutant General (1793); Secretary of Education (1837); Insurance Commissioner (1873); Secretary of Banking (1891); Secretary of Agriculture (1895); Secretary of Health (1905); State Police Commissioner (1905); Secretary of Labor and Industry (1913); Secretary of Public Welfare (1921); Secretary of Revenue (1927); Secretary of Commerce (1939); Secretary of Community Affairs (1966); Secretary of Transportation (1970); Secretary of Environmental Resources (1970); Secretary of General Services (1975); Secretary of Aging (1978); and Corrections Commissioner (1984).

The formation of additional cabinet-level agencies can come as a result of a request from the Governor or through the initiative of the General Assembly. In either case, any proposed additions to the cabinet must be approved by the General Assembly.

The reverse is true also. The elimination of a cabinet-level agency must be approved by the General Assembly, whether the action is proposed by the Governor or the General Assembly.

146. WHAT ARE THE OFFICIAL DUTIES OF THE CABINET?

Cabinet members are the Governor's regular advisors and meet at the Governor's call.

The Administrative Code establishes the departments that the cabinet members head and outlines their powers and duties.

147. WHAT IF THERE IS A TIE VOTE IN ELECTING THE GOVERNOR?

In the unlikely event that a popular vote for Governor ends in a tie, the winner would be chosen by a joint vote of the members of both houses of the General Assembly.

148. *ARE THERE ANY RESTRICTIONS ON WHO CAN SERVE AS GOVERNOR OR LIEUTENANT GOVERNOR?*

Yes. Under the Constitution, no member of Congress or anyone holding any office under the United States or the Commonwealth of Pennsylvania can serve as Governor or Lieutenant Governor (see Article IV, Section 6).

The Governor and Lieutenant Governor must be citizens of the United States, at least 30 years old, and have lived in the Commonwealth at least seven years preceding his or her election.

149. *BEYOND CABINET MEMBERS AND THE BOARD OF PARDONS, CAN THE GOVERNOR MAKE ANY OTHER APPOINTMENTS?*

Yes. The Constitution provides for the appointment of a Secretary of Education and such other officers as allowed by law, subject to the consent of a two-thirds majority of the Senate (see Article IV, Section 8).

150. *WHO IS THE COMMANDER-IN-CHIEF OF THE COMMONWEALTH'S MILITARY FORCES?*

The Governor is commander-in-chief of Pennsylvania's military forces except when they are called into United States service.

151. *CAN THE GOVERNOR GRANT PARDONS?*

Yes. The Governor has the power to remit fines and forfeitures, grant reprieves, commute sentences, and grant pardons in all criminal cases except impeachment. However, the Governor cannot grant a pardon or commute a sentence without a written recommendation from the majority of the Board of Pardons after a full hearing in open session.

152. WHO ARE THE MEMBERS OF THE BOARD OF PARDONS?

The Board of Pardons is chaired by the Lieutenant Governor and also includes the Attorney General and three members appointed by the Governor with the consent of a two-thirds majority of the Senate.

Of the three appointees, one must be a member of the bar, one a penologist, and one a physician; all must be Pennsylvania residents. They are appointed for a six-year term.

153. CAN THE GOVERNOR FILL VACANCIES IN OFFICES?

Yes. The Constitution gives the Governor power to make appointments to fill vacancies in offices (see Article IV, Section 8).

154. WHAT IS THE PROCEDURE FOR FILLING THESE VACANCIES?

The Governor must make a nomination to the Senate within 90 days of the vacancy. The Senate must act on the nomination within 25 legislative days (days of actual session).

155. WHAT IF THE SENATE IS IN RECESS OR HAS ADJOURNED?

If the Governor makes a nomination to fill a vacancy during a recess or after adjournment, the Senate must act on it within 25 legislative days after returning or reconvening.

If the body fails to act within the 25 days, the nominee takes office without consent of the Senate.

Pennsylvania's unified judicial system means that every court in the Commonwealth is under the supervision of the state Supreme Court. The judicial system may be thought of as a pyramid, with the Supreme Court at the apex. Below it are the two appellate courts, Superior Court and Commonwealth Court, followed by the Courts of Common Pleas. The base of the pyramid is the minor judiciary of the community courts, district justices, the municipal and traffic courts of Philadelphia, and Pittsburgh's police magistrate courts.

The citizens of Pennsylvania depend on the judicial system to interpret and apply the laws of our Commonwealth. It is a great responsibility and a very important one in terms of maintaining order and justice in our state.

This section examines the various jurisdictions of Pennsylvania's courts and the responsibilities and restrictions of the judges and justices of those courts.

156. How does the Constitution provide for judicial power?

The fifth article of the Constitution vests judicial power of the Commonwealth in a "unified judicial system consisting of the Supreme Court, the Superior Court, the Commonwealth Court, Courts of Common Pleas, community courts, municipal and traffic courts in the City of Philadelphia" and other courts as provided by law and justices of the peace.

157. How is the unified judicial system administered?

The Administrative Office of Pennsylvania Courts oversees the unified judicial system and is responsible for the prompt and proper disposition of the business of all courts. A court administrator heads the office and is appointed by the Supreme Court.

158. What is the difference between Supreme, Superior, and Commonwealth Courts?

Aside from differences in jurisdiction, the primary distinction is that the Supreme Court is part of the constitutional framework of Pennsylvania's state government. Both the Superior and Commonwealth Courts were established by an act of the General Assembly.

The Supreme Court is Pennsylvania's highest court and holds the Commonwealth's supreme judicial power. It makes the final judgment on interpreting the Constitution in regard to statutes enacted by the General Assembly.

THE SUPREME COURT

159. What is the jurisdiction of the Supreme Court?

The Supreme Court has original but not exclusive jurisdiction over:

a) all cases of *habeas corpus* (any of several common law writs issued to bring a party before a court or judge);

b) all cases of *mandamus* (a command by a superior court for the performance of a specified official act or duty) or prohibition to courts of inferior jurisdiction; and

c) all cases of *quo warranto* as to any officer of statewide jurisdiction (requiring demonstration of the authority by which an individual exercises a public office).

The Supreme Court has exclusive jurisdiction of appeals from final orders of the Courts of Common Pleas in cases of:

a) felony murder;

b) the right to public office;

c) matters decided in the orphans' court division;

d) certain actions or proceedings in equity;

e) direct criminal contempt in the Courts of Common Pleas and other contempt proceedings relating to orders appealable directly to the Court;

f) suspension or disbarment from the practice of law and other related disciplinary orders or sanctions;

g) supersession of a District Attorney by an Attorney General or a court;

h) matters in which the right or power of the Commonwealth or any political subdivision to create or issue indebtedness is in question; and

i) rulings of unconstitutionality by a Court of Common Pleas.

The Supreme Court has exclusive jurisdiction of appeals from all final orders of the Commonwealth Court, provided the matter was originally commenced in that court and not as an appeal from another court, an administrative agency, or justice of the peace. (One exception is an appeal to a final order of the Commonwealth Court that was made on an appeal from the Board of Finance and Revenue.)

The Supreme Court can review certain final orders of the Superior and Commonwealth Courts if any party to the matter petitions the court and an appeal is granted by any two justices.

In addition, the Court can assume full jurisdiction over any matter involving an issue of immediate public importance pending before any court or justice of the peace in the Commonwealth, either on its own motion or upon petition of any party.

160. HOW MANY JUSTICES ARE THERE ON THE SUPREME COURT?

Seven, with one serving as Chief Justice.

161. HOW IS THE CHIEF JUSTICE CHOSEN?

The Chief Justice is chosen on the basis of longest continuous service, or seniority.

162. IF TWO JUSTICES ARE ELECTED AT THE SAME TIME, HOW IS SENIORITY DETERMINED?

If two justices are elected at the same time, they draw lots to decide who has seniority.

As in all of Pennsylvania's courts, elected justices have seniority over appointed ones.

163. How are Supreme Court Justices chosen?

Justices are elected by the voters.

164. What is the term of office of a Supreme Court Justice?

Justices are elected for a term of 10 years, after which they are eligible for retention election.

165. How is a Supreme Court Justice retained?

A justice must file a declaration of candidacy for retention election no later than the first Monday of January in the year before the current term expires.

If no declaration is filed, a vacancy will exist upon expiration of the justice's term. If a declaration is filed, the justice's name (without party designation) will then be submitted to electors at the municipal election immediately preceding the expiration of the term to determine if the justice will be retained in office.

A majority vote in favor will retain the justice for another term of office. If a majority is against retention, a vacancy will exist and be filled by appointment at the expiration of the justice's current term.

166. How is a vacancy on the Supreme Court filled?

The Governor makes an appointment to fill any vacancy on the Supreme Court, and the appointee must be confirmed by a two-thirds vote of the Senate.

167. Does the Pennsylvania Supreme Court sit in any city other than Harrisburg?

Yes, it also sits in Philadelphia and Pittsburgh. In order to expedite the business of the court, the Commonwealth is divided into three districts.

The Eastern District, with a prothonotary's office in Philadelphia, includes the counties of Bedford, Berks, Bradford, Bucks, Cameron, Carbon, Centre, Chester, Clinton, Columbia, Cumberland, Delaware, Elk, Huntingdon, Juniata, Lackawanna, Lancaster, Lebanon, Lehigh, Luzerne, Lycoming, Monroe, Montgomery, Montour, Northampton, Northumberland, Philadelphia, Pike, Potter, Schuylkill, Snyder, Sullivan, Susquehanna, Tioga, Union, Wayne, and Wyoming.

The Middle District, with a prothonotary's office in Harrisburg, includes Adams, Dauphin, Franklin, Fulton, Mifflin, Perry, and York counties.

The Western District, with a prothonotary's office in Pittsburgh, includes the remaining counties of Allegheny, Armstrong, Beaver, Blair, Butler, Cambria, Clarion, Clearfield, Crawford, Erie, Fayette, Forest, Greene, Indiana, Jefferson, Lawrence, McKean, Mercer, Somerset, Venango, Warren, Washington, and Westmoreland.

168. HOW MANY SESSIONS OF THE SUPREME COURT ARE HELD EACH YEAR?

Eight. Supreme Court Rule 26 provides for regular sessions to be held in Philadelphia during winter, spring, and fall for the Eastern District; in Harrisburg during the spring for the Middle District; and in Pittsburgh during spring and fall for the Western District.

169. HOW ARE THE SESSION DATES ESTABLISHED?

The dates are fixed by court calendars.

170. WHO WAS THE FIRST CHIEF JUSTICE OF THE PENNSYLVANIA SUPREME COURT?

William Penn appointed Captain William Crispin as the first Chief Justice in a letter dated August 18, 1681. Crispin died at sea on his way to Pennsylvania.

The first Chief Justice to fulfill his duties was Dr. Nicholas Moore, who undertook the position on June 4, 1684.

SUPERIOR COURT

171. WHAT IS THE JURISDICTION OF THE SUPERIOR COURT?

The Superior Court has exclusive jurisdiction over appeals from the Courts of Common Pleas, except for those types of appeals under exclusive jurisdiction of the Supreme or Commonwealth Courts.

The Superior Court has original jurisdiction to entertain, hold hearings on, and decide applications for wiretapping and electronic surveillance.

172. WHEN WAS THE SUPERIOR COURT ESTABLISHED?

The Superior Court was established by legislation approved by the Governor in June 1895. The 1968 Constitutional Convention made it a constitutional court.

173. HOW MANY JUDGES ARE ON THE SUPERIOR COURT?

There are 15, with one serving as President Judge, who in addition to judicial duties, is responsible for assigning cases.

174. HOW IS THE PRESIDENT JUDGE CHOSEN?

The first President Judge was determined by the drawing of lots. After that, the President Judge was chosen on the basis of seniority. If two or more judges were elected at the same time, they would draw lots to decide seniority.

Since 1985, however, the President Judge has been elected by a majority vote of the judges of the court for a five-year term. After serving a full five-year term, no President Judge can be re-elected without there being an intervening full elected term.

175. How are judges of the Superior Court chosen and what is their term of office?

Like the members of the Supreme Court, they are chosen in a municipal election. The terms and conditions for their re-election are also the same as for justices of the Supreme Court. (See questions 163, 164, and 165.)

176. How is a vacancy on the Superior Court filled?

In the same manner as the Supreme Court. (See question 166.)

177. Does the Pennsylvania Superior Court sit in any city other than Harrisburg?

Yes, in Philadelphia and Pittsburgh. The state is divided into the Philadelphia District, the Harrisburg District, and the Pittsburgh District. These districts have the same composition as the Eastern, Middle, and Western Districts of the Supreme Court. (See question 167.)

In addition, upon the joint invitation of the judges of a county Court of Common Pleas and that county's bar association, the Superior Court periodically holds special sessions in other cities.

178. How many sessions of the Superior Court are held each year?

The Superior Court holds no preset number of sessions. The Court ordinarily sits in panels of three judges, whose composition changes weekly. The number of argument sessions conducted each year is determined by the number of appeals filed.

In addition, appeals submitted without oral argument are considered by three-judge panels.

Periodically, the Court sits in *en banc* sessions (in which the entire court participates) commonly three to six times each year.

179. WHO WAS THE FIRST PRESIDENT JUDGE OF THE SUPERIOR COURT?

Charles E. Rice of Wilkes-Barre, Luzerne County, became the first President Judge on June 28, 1895.

COMMONWEALTH COURT

180. WHAT IS THE JURISDICTION OF THE COMMONWEALTH COURT?

The Commonwealth Court is primarily an appellate court, but it does have some original jurisdiction.

It has exclusive appellate jurisdiction of:

a) final orders of the Courts of Common Pleas in certain specific cases;

b) final orders of Commonwealth agencies including appeals from the Environmental Hearing Board, Public Utility Commission, Unemployment Compensation Board of Review, and any other Commonwealth agency having statewide authority, with certain specific exceptions;

c) awards of arbitrators in disputes between the Commonwealth and a state employee; and

d) any other matter as set by statute.

The Commonwealth Court also has original jurisdiction of:

a) all civil actions or proceedings against state government, including, with some exceptions, any state officer acting in an official capacity;

b) all civil actions by state government or an officer of it except eminent domain;

c) all civil actions under certain provisions of the Insurance Department Act of 1921;

d) election matters relating to statewide offices; and

e) any other matter as determined by statute.

181. HOW MANY JUDGES ARE ON THE COMMONWEALTH COURT?

Nine, with one serving as President Judge. The Supreme Court also designates six senior judges to sit with the Commonwealth Court.

182. HOW IS THE PRESIDENT JUDGE CHOSEN?

The judges of the court elect a President Judge for a term of five years.

183. WHAT IS THE TERM OF OFFICE OF A JUDGE OF THE COMMONWEALTH COURT?

A judge of the Commonwealth Court is elected to serve a 10-year term. At the end of a term, a judge may run for retention and serve another 10 years.

184. DOES THE COMMONWEALTH COURT SIT IN ANY CITY OTHER THAN HARRISBURG?

Yes. The court holds regular sessions in Philadelphia and Pittsburgh in addition to Harrisburg. Special sessions may be held in any judicial district of the state when deemed to be in the interest of justice, for the convenience of parties and/or witnesses, or for any other reason.

185. HOW MANY SESSIONS OF THE COMMONWEALTH COURT ARE HELD EACH YEAR?

Nine. The court conducts regular sessions each month except in January, July, and August.

PHILADELPHIA MUNICIPAL AND TRAFFIC COURTS

186. WHAT IS THE JURISDICTION OF THE MUNICIPAL COURT OF PHILADELPHIA?

The criminal jurisdiction of the Municipal Court of Philadelphia includes:

- summary offenses except those under motor vehicle law;

- all criminal offenses in which no prison term can be imposed or which are punishable by imprisonment of no more than five years; and

- certain more serious offenses under motor vehicle law.

In civil cases, the court has jurisdiction in:

- landlord and tenant matters;

- damage from breach of agreement, recovering damages for breach of contract or promise;

- trespass claims involving no more than $5,000; and

- actions for fines and penalties by a governmental agency involving $5,000 or less (exclusive of interest and costs) or in matters concerning local taxes, up to $15,000.

In any of these criminal or civil cases, the defendant has no right of trial by jury in this court but can appeal to the Court of Common Pleas for a new trial and does have the right to trial by jury there.

187. *W*HEN WAS THE *T*RAFFIC *C*OURT OF
    *P*HILADELPHIA ESTABLISHED*?*

> The Traffic Court of Philadelphia, established by Act 106, was approved by the Governor on October 17, 1969.

188. *H*OW MANY JUDGES ARE ASSIGNED TO THE *T*RAFFIC
    *C*OURT OF *P*HILADELPHIA*?*

> Six judges are appointed by the Governor, who also names one of the six to be President Judge.

189. *W*HAT IS THE JURISDICTION OF THE *T*RAFFIC
    *C*OURT OF *P*HILADELPHIA*?*

> It has exclusive jurisdiction of all summary offenses under Title 75 of the state motor vehicle laws and the violation of any motor vehicle ordinance committed within Philadelphia County.

DISTRICT JUSTICES

190. *W*HEN WERE THE JUSTICES OF THE PEACE
    ESTABLISHED AND HOW HAVE THEY EVOLVED*?*

> The Constitution of 1776 provided for justices of the peace—now called district justices—to be elected by the freeholders of each city and county respectively. Two or more could be elected for a seven-year term, but the General Assembly could remove them for misconduct.
>
> The Constitution of 1874 called for the election of justices of the peace when constables were elected, and the Governor was now to commission them for a five-year term. No ward, district, borough, or township could elect more than two justices without the electors' consent. This Constitution also established a residency requirement of one year preceding the election.

In 1909, a constitutional amendment required the election of justices of the peace through a municipal election and changed the term of office from five to six years.

A 1968 constitutional amendment abolished all this, except for the residency requirement. The amendment provided that in any judicial district—other than the City of Philadelphia—where no community court exists, there shall be one justice of the peace in each magisterial district (see Article V, Section 7(a)).

Since the adoption of this amendment and the passage of subsequent legislation, justices of the peace are now referred to as district justices.

191 WHAT IS THE JURISDICTION OF DISTRICT JUSTICES?

In general, district justices have jurisdiction over the following matters:

1) summary offenses, except those within the jurisdiction of a traffic court;

2) certain matters arising under the Landlord and Tenant Act of 1951;

3) certain civil claims (except by or against a Commonwealth party) in which the sum demanded does not exceed $4,000;

4) as commissioners to preside at arraignments, fix and accept bail, issue warrants, and perform duties of a similar nature;

5) offenses relating to driving under the influence of alcohol or controlled substance, within specific criteria;

6) misdemeanors of the third degree, within specific criteria and with certain exceptions, under Title 18 (crimes and offenses) and Title 30 (fish);

7) all offenses under Title 34 (game); and

8) any other matter for which district justices have jurisdiction by statute.

192. *What is the training and instruction course for district justices required by the Constitution?*

District justices must complete a course of training and instruction in the duties of their office and pass an examination prior to assuming office.

The course cannot be any longer than four weeks and consists of at least 40 hours of class instruction in civil and criminal law. Topics include evidence, procedure, summary proceedings, and laws relating to motor vehicles. In addition, every district justice must attend at least one continuing education program practicum course each year.

The Minor Judiciary Education Board prescribes and approves the subject matter and examination for the course of training and instruction as well as the subject matter of practicum courses.

193. *How are the magisterial districts established?*

The General Assembly establishes the classes of magisterial districts based on population.

194. *How are the number and boundaries of magisterial districts determined?*

These are determined by the Pennsylvania Supreme Court or by the Courts of Common Pleas under the direction of the Supreme Court.

195. *How many magisterial districts are there?*

As of March 1994, there were 550 districts.

196. *When were these judicial districts formed?*

Act 106 established judicial districts in 1931.

The Judicial Code, derived from the Pennsylvania Constitution, was amended in 1982 to provide for the establishment of 60 judicial districts, composed of one or more counties, within the state. This code also specifies the number for each district.

197. *How can judicial districts be changed?*

According to the Constitution, the number and boundaries of judicial districts can be changed by the General Assembly only with the advice and consent of the Supreme Court (see Article V, Section 11).

COURTS OF COMMON PLEAS

198. *What is the jurisdiction of the Courts of Common Pleas?*

Except where an exclusive original jurisdiction is vested in another court, the Courts of Common Pleas have unlimited original jurisdiction of all civil and criminal actions and proceedings.

Their jurisdiction includes:

- appeals from final orders of the district's minor judiciary (also called justice of the peace);

- appeals from state agencies, such as matters relating to motor vehicle violations, liquor code violations, birth and death records, inheritance and estate taxes, occupational disease, and public employee disputes; and

- petitions for review of awards by arbitrators in disputes between local government agencies and their employees.

There must be at least one Court of Common Pleas in each judicial district, and each judicial district has a President Judge. Courts with eight or more judges elect a President Judge for a non-successive, five-year term. In courts with fewer judges, the judge with the longest continuous service is appointed President Judge.

All districts have a trial division within the Court of Common Pleas, and larger counties have other divisions as well. The divisions are administrative units composed of judges who are responsible for specific types of court business. Each division is presided over by an administrative judge who assists the President Judge.

199. WHAT IS THE JURISDICTION OF THE COURT OF COMMON PLEAS OF PHILADELPHIA COUNTY?

The Court of Common Pleas of Philadelphia County has three divisions.

The Trial Division has jurisdiction over criminal and civil matters.

The Orphans' Court Division has jurisdiction over all adoptions, custody of minors, and numerous other matters.

The Family Court Division has exclusive jurisdiction in adoptions and delayed birth certificates. It also has jurisdiction in domestic relations matters such as desertion or non-payment of support, child custody, divorce, and delinquent children.

200. WHAT IS THE JURISDICTION OF THE COURT OF COMMON PLEAS OF ALLEGHENY COUNTY?

The Court of Common Pleas of Allegheny County consists of four divisions: the Civil Division, the Criminal Division, Orphans' Court, and Family Court.

The jurisdiction of these divisions is very similar to the divisions of the Philadelphia court, except that Philadelphia's Trial Division handles all the matters included in Allegheny County's separate Civil and Criminal Divisions.

201. WHAT OTHER COURTS ARE THERE IN ALLEGHENY COUNTY?

Pittsburgh's police magistrate courts are a unique part of the unified judicial system and are the only city courts in the state. Six judges are appointed by the Mayor of Pittsburgh to serve during the same term of office. These are the only Pennsylvania judges not elected to office.

202. WHAT IS THE JURISDICTION OF PITTSBURGH'S POLICE MAGISTRATE COURTS?

Jurisdiction of these courts roughly parallels that of the district justices except that its functions are limited within the boundaries of the City of Pittsburgh. Judges of these courts also serve in the city's traffic and housing courts.

203. WHAT COURTS ARE KNOWN AS THE "MINOR JUDICIARY"?

The minor judiciary includes community courts, district justices, Philadelphia Municipal Court, Pittsburgh police magistrate courts, and the Philadelphia Traffic Court.